The Christmas Truce of WORLD WAR I

written by Nel Yomtov
illustrated by János Orbán

raintree
a Capstone company — publishers for children

The author wishes to dedicate this book to his granddaughters, Jamie Shea and Nina Raye.

Raintree is an imprint of Capstone Global Library Limited, a company incorporated in England and Wales having its registered office at 264 Banbury Road, Oxford, OX2 7DY – Registered company number: 6695582

www.raintree.co.uk
myorders@raintree.co.uk

Copyright © 2025 Capstone Global Library Limited
The moral rights of the proprietor have been asserted.

All rights reserved. No part of this publication may be reproduced in any form or by any means (including photocopying or storing it in any medium by electronic means and whether or not transiently or incidentally to some other use of this publication) without the written permission of the copyright owner, except in accordance with the provisions of the Copyright, Designs and Patents Act 1988 or under the terms of a licence issued by the Copyright Licensing Agency, 5th Floor, Shackleton House, 4 Battle Bridge Lane, London SE1 2HX (www.cla.co.uk). Applications for the copyright owner's written permission should be addressed to the publisher.

Editorial credits
Edited by Christopher Harbo
Designed by Tracy Davies
Production by Katy LaVigne
Printed and bound in India
Design Element: Shutterstock/kzww

Direct quotations appear in bold italicized text on the following pages: Pages 13, 21; 22 from *Christmas Truce* by Malcolm Brown and Shirley Seaton (Pan Books, 1994). Page 19 from "WWI's Christmas Truce: When Fighting Paused for the Holiday" by A.J. Baime and Volker Janssen (history.com, October 29, 2018). Page 23 from *The Christmas Truce* by Terri Blom Crocker (University of Kentucky Press, 2017). Page 27 from a letter by Captain "Jake" Armes of the 1st Battalion North Staffordshire Regiment (lettersofnote.com, October 19, 2015).

978 1 3982 5831 0

British Library Cataloguing in Publication Data
A full catalogue record for this book is available from the British Library.

All product and company names are trademarks™ or registered® trademarks of their respective holders.

All the internet addresses (URLs) given in this book were valid at the time of going to press. However, due to the dynamic nature of the internet, some addresses may have changed, or sites may have changed or ceased to exist since publication. While the author and publisher regret any inconvenience this may cause readers, no responsibility for any such changes can be accepted by either the author or the publisher.

Contents

Introduction
The world at war 4

Chapter 1
Prelude to peace 6

Chapter 2
An evening to remember 10

Chapter 3
"The most extraordinary Christmas" 16

Chapter 4
How it ended 22

Chapter 5
The legendary Christmas Truce 26

More about the Christmas Truce 28
Glossary 30
Find out more 31
About the author 32
About the illustrator 32

Introduction THE WORLD AT WAR

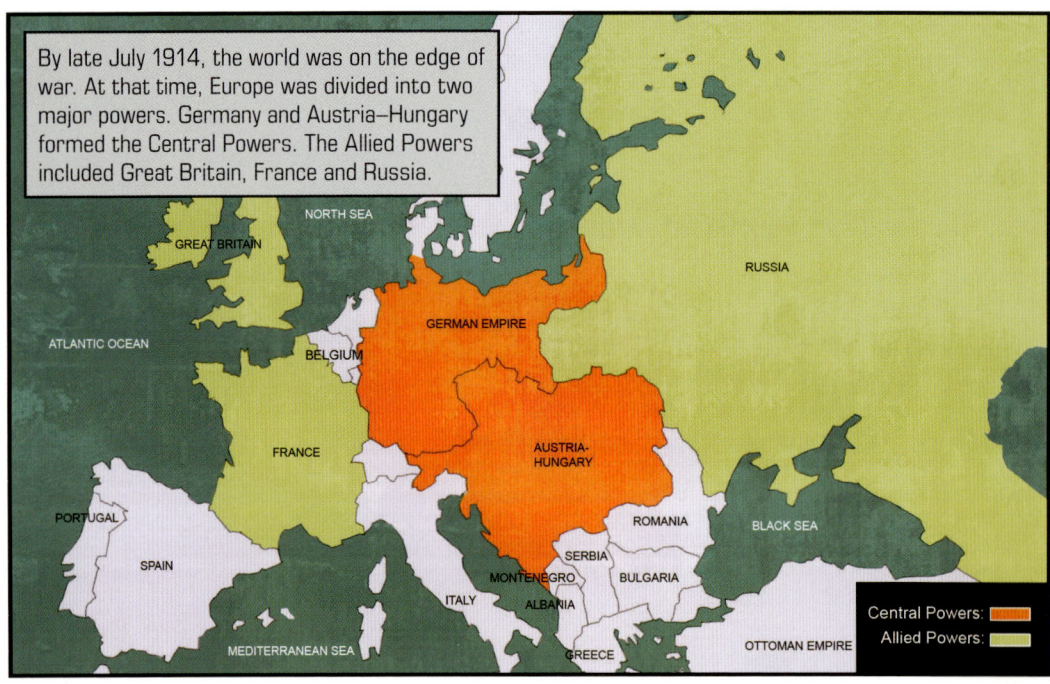

By late July 1914, the world was on the edge of war. At that time, Europe was divided into two major powers. Germany and Austria–Hungary formed the Central Powers. The Allied Powers included Great Britain, France and Russia.

In early August, Germany invaded Belgium. Weeks later, German troops smashed into France from the north. In October, the Ottoman Empire joined the Central Powers.

By November, both sides were locked in a stalemate.

In only four months of fighting, nearly 400,000 soldiers were killed or wounded.

The two armies dug long, deep trenches. The Western Front's trench line ran along northern France and Belgium. In many places, the opposing armies were only about 35 metres apart.

The ground between the armies was called No Man's Land.

Meanwhile, each side waged a campaign of hatred against the other.

British newspapers said Germans were savages set on devastation and destruction.

German newspapers claimed Britain was a threat to mankind and urged readers to hate the British.

Yet, as Christmas 1914 approached, one of the most humane events in the history of warfare was about to take place.

Chapter 1 **PRELUDE TO PEACE**

For many of the fighting nations, Christmas was a festive time filled with spiritual and religious importance.

Many Christmas customs started in Germany. The Christmas tree – or *Tannenbaum* – had been popular since the early 1600s.

Christmas carols and the tradition of Santa Claus were also important in Germany.

But both sides celebrated these customs.

As Christmas approached, Allied soldiers started getting warm clothing, medicines, watches and other goodies from home.

"A gold watch from good ol' Granny!"

"Butterscotch from me mum! Have some, boys!"

Chapter 2 AN EVENING TO REMEMBER

Days before Christmas, along the trench line . . .

"It's got colder, but the rain has finally stopped, Conrad."

"Yes, Ivan. It's a good sign from heaven, especially as Christmas is coming."

Western Front Trench, December 1914

French/British side
- Ypres
- Wytschoete
- Messines
- Ploegsteert
- Lys River
- Bois-Grenier
- Neuve Chappelle
- Givenchy
- La Bassée
- Hulluch

German side

Late in the afternoon on Christmas Eve . . .

"Quickly, Conrad. Light those candles! The celebration begins now!"

"Be careful when you put up your tree. The Englishmen may start shooting."

10

Chapter 3 "THE MOST EXTRAORDINARY CHRISTMAS"

Many photographs were taken that Christmas Day. For the first time in the history of war, enemies were shown standing cheerfully side by side.

Chapter 4 HOW IT ENDED

Reports of the holiday truce appeared in newspapers one week after Christmas. The reports were based on letters from soldiers.

In the *London Times*, a British general said the Germans **"are jolly, cheery fellows for the most part"**. He also wrote it seemed **"so silly under the circumstances to be fighting them"**.

Some German newspapers also reported the truce. In response, the German army warned that any future friendly contact with the enemy **"will be punished as treason"**.

Chapter 5   THE LEGENDARY CHRISTMAS TRUCE

Christmas 1914 was an astounding event. For a brief time, young soldiers let go of the hatred they'd been fed by their governments.

They discovered their enemies were not monsters. They were men – like themselves. Only by fate had they found themselves on opposite ends of a rifle.

For some men, the truce was simply a time for fun and games – a brief break from the gruesome war.

Others enjoyed the truce as a way of disobeying orders when the high command wasn't looking.

For many, the truce was a small glimmer of hope that the war would end soon.

Over time, the Christmas truce took on legendary status. Across Belgium and France, many monuments were created to recall that famous day.

For, as one soldier described it best, ***"it will be a thing to remember all one's life"***.

MORE ABOUT THE CHRISTMAS TRUCE

- In December 1914, the trench line ran for 32 kilometres, from Ypres, Belgium, to La Bassee Canal in northern France. The truce occurred along 24 kilometres of the line. More than 100,000 soldiers participated in the truce. In time, the trenches would stretch from the English Channel in the north to the Swiss Alps in the south – a distance of about 765 kilometres.

- The friendly contact and ease of communication between the enemy armies was possible because many Germans spoke English. Many had worked in Britain as waiters, porters, bakers, butchers and barbers in the years before the war.

- Unlike the British, Belgian and French soldiers did not mingle much with the Germans during the truce. After all, Belgium and France had been seized by the Germans. To have friendly contact with the Germans would be an act of treason.

- Although the truce involved more than three-quarters of the entire trench line, fighting in some areas occurred. At various points up and down the trench line, snipers still kept busy.

- Despite warnings from high command, very few soldiers on either side were punished for participating in the truce. The commanders eventually realized the truce was not a rebellion but instead a reaction to the horrid conditions of warfare and the closeness of the enemy. Through it all, soldiers on both sides were professionals who supported the war and fought to defeat the enemy.

- World War I (1914–1918) ended on 11 November 1918, when Germany officially surrendered in the presence of representatives of the governments of Britain, France and Germany. More than 30 million soldiers were killed or wounded in the fighting, and nearly 8 million civilians lost their lives.

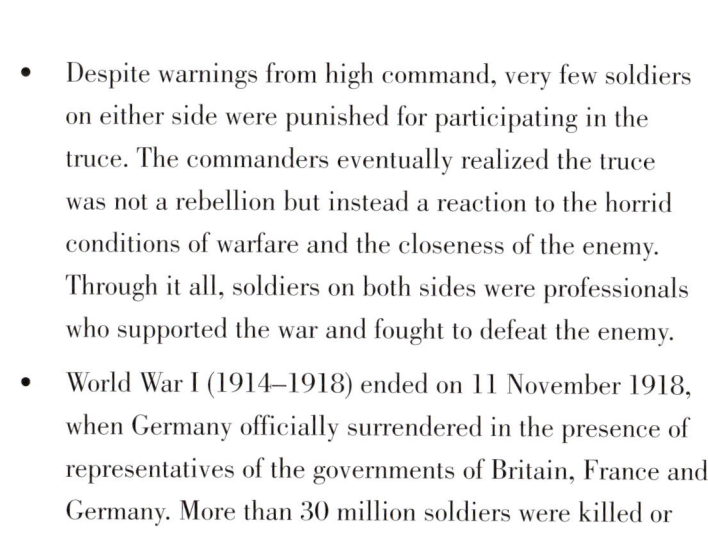

GLOSSARY

Allied Powers group of countries that fought the Central powers in World War I; the Allies included Britain, the United States, France, Russia and Italy

campaign series of battles fought in one region

Central Powers group of countries that fought the Allied Powers in World War I; the Central Powers included Germany, Turkey and Austria–Hungary

chaplain minister, priest or rabbi who performs religious ceremonies and advises people in the military

custom tradition in a culture or society

discipline punish someone formally for breaking a rule or law

homage special honour or respect shown publicly

humane kind and charitable

Ottoman Empire Turkish empire in south-eastern Europe, western Asia and northern Africa that was founded in 1300 and ruled over until after World War I

rebellion fight against the people in charge

resolution firm decision to do something

sniper soldier trained to shoot at long-distance targets from a hidden place

stalemate situation in which neither side of opposing forces can win

treason crime of betraying your country

trench long, deep area dug into the ground with soil piled up on one side for defence

truce temporary agreement to stop fighting

FIND OUT MORE

Books

Cher Ami Comes Through: Heroic Carrier Pigeon of World War I, Nel Yomtov (Raintree, 2023)

War Horse, Michael Morpurgo (Farshore, 2023)

World War I (DK Eyewitness), DK (DK Children, 2023)

Websites

kids.britannica.com/kids/article/The-Christmas-Truce/607325
Read more about the Christmas Truce with Britannica Kids.

www.youtube.com/watch?v=Fk-LjY16zdM
This video tells the story of the Christmas Truce.

www.twinkl.co.uk/teaching-wiki/the-christmas-truce-of-1914
Find out lots more about the Christmas Truce on this website.

ABOUT THE AUTHOR

Nel Yomtov is an award-winning author of children's non-fiction books and graphic novels. He specializes in writing about history, current events, biography, architecture and military history. He has written numerous graphic novels, including *Raising the Flag on Iwo Jima*, *School Strike for Climate* and *Cher Ami: Heroic Carrier Pigeon of World War I*. In 2020, he self-published *Baseball 100*, an illustrated book featuring the 100 greatest players in baseball history. Nel lives in New York City, USA.
Author photo by Nancy Golden

ABOUT THE ILLUSTRATOR

János Orbán grew up in Budapest, Hungary, where his love of art began at an early age. After graduating from an art secondary school, he went on to earn a degree from the Hungarian University of Fine Arts. With a passion for illustration, János most enjoys designing characters and creating artwork for children's books. He has two daughters and a son, and he currently lives and works with his family in a village near Budapest.
Illustrator photo by János Orbán